asticine—a few pieces.

me tin-tacks.

four-inch nail. Some two-
ch nails.

large needle or bodkin.

small cork.

small glass jar.

clothes peg.

n filings—1oz. or less.

pper sulphate crystals.

me drawing-pins and paper
ps.

e or two small pieces of
od.

Series 621

With simple text and fascinating coloured illustrations this Ladybird Science Book introduces a child to the principles of electricity and magnetism.

This vital subject is explained by simple experiments and working models a child can make with easily obtained materials, and with complete safety. Step by step the young reader learns the fundamental principles in a most enjoyable and thoroughly practical manner. It is the perfect introduction to science, and to the scientific way of thinking.

The electrical experiments in this book are done with torch batteries, and are therefore all perfectly safe.

Under no circumstances should you ever attempt to experiment with electricity from the mains, or with mains switches, plugs or lamp sockets.

The Publishers wish to acknowledge the helpful interest and encouragement given by J. Cottam, Dip.Ed. (Headmaster) in the early stages of planning this series.

A Ladybird Junior Science Book

MAGNETS, BULBS and BATTERIES

by F. E. NEWING, B.Sc.
and RICHARD BOWOOD

with illustrations by
J. H. WINGFIELD

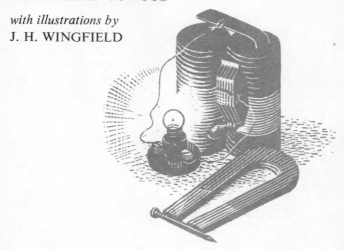

Publishers: Ladybird Books Ltd . Loughborough
© Ladybird Books Ltd (formerly Wills & Hepworth Ltd) 1962
Printed in England

Finding out by Experiment

You can do all these experiments with very simple apparatus. If you do them carefully, they should work first time. If you are not successful first time do not be disappointed. Find out *why;* there is always a reason.

The girl in the picture has found that her lamp does not light. Her brother is helping her to find out why, so that she can mend it. First they try another battery, but still it does not light. They try another bulb, but with no success. Next they look at the switch, and find the cause of the trouble. The switch is dirty, and is not making a good contact. They clean it with sandpaper, put the lamp together—and it lights!

They have solved their problem by *trial and error,* which is very much the way the scientist works in his laboratory. He thinks about a problem, tries to find the answer by experiment, and if he does not succeed he goes on trying different ways until his problem is solved.

If one of your experiments does not work, find out why. Look first to make sure that all the connections are good — tight and clean. Correct any fault you find, and try again.

From these experiments you will be able to find out for yourself something about electricity and magnetism.

4

Magnets

There is a close connection between electricity and magnetism, so shall we start with some experiments with magnets?

If you have not got a magnet you can buy one quite cheaply at an ironmongers. Collect all sorts of small things; the picture will give you some ideas. Scatter them about the table and begin your experiment.

Bring your magnet close to each of the articles in turn, to see which are attracted and which are not. Test everything several times, to make sure the result is not an accident. Make a list of the things your magnet attracts, and a list of the others.

When you have tested everything, look at your lists. You will have found out something. A magnet only strongly attracts iron or steel, or articles which contain iron or steel.

If you can get two or more magnets, perhaps one of them a straight or *bar magnet*, test them in turn with a packet of tintacks. You can find how strong a magnet is by the number of tintacks it picks up. You may also find that a small magnet can be stronger than a larger one.

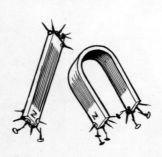

You will have noticed something else. The tintacks cluster round the ends, called the *poles*, of a magnet.

6

Using Magnets

The children in the picture are using magnets to steer ships. They have made two little ships from corks, with match-stick masts and paper sails, and enough tintacks in the bottom to make them float upright.

The ships float on water in a plastic tray standing on blocks. By holding the magnets underneath the tray the children can move the ships about.

If you have got one magnet you can use it to make others. To make a lasting magnet use steel, because iron will not stay magnetised.

This is how you do it. Take a piece of steel, such as a steel knitting or darning needle, or a piece of old clock spring. Stroke it with one pole of your magnet, always in the same direction, and lifting the magnet well clear at the end of each stroke. You will find that the steel you are stroking will soon become a magnet and will itself attract iron or steel.

You do not "use up" a magnet when you make others with it. You only spoil a magnet with rough use, by making it hot or by leaving off the "keeper", the piece of iron across the poles when it is not in use. An iron nail is a good keeper.

Making a Compass

When you have magnetised a needle, you can make a compass. You need a small flat cork (or a round slice of cork) and a saucer with some water in it.

Lay the needle on the cork, and float it in the saucer of water. Watch it. It will turn to point one way. Take it out and put it in the water several times, pointing in different directions. If you have magnetised the needle, it will always turn to point the same way.

The needle points North and South. To be exact, one end points to the *Magnetic North*, which is nearly the same as true North. Ask someone which is the North from where you are, and see which end of the needle points that way. Next mark a piece of paper with the *points of the compass*, and put it underneath the saucer—as in the picture. Turn the paper until the North mark is in the same direction as the north end of your needle. There you have a compass.

You can make another compass by magnetising a steel knitting needle. Hang it from a pencil by a thin thread in a paper "stirrup". That too will turn to point North and South.

Always keep other magnets well away from the compass, or they will affect the direction the needle points.

Making a Lighthouse

Now we will use electricity, and make a model lighthouse which lights up. The lighthouse itself is made from an empty carton (such as a salt container) which you paint in stripes. Mount the carton on a wooden base with plasticine (with which you can also mould some rocks). A small glass fish-paste jar makes the lamp-house.

To make the light you need a torch battery, a small bulb, a bulb holder and some very thin bell wire. If the battery is marked "3V" it means that it is a 3 volt battery, which needs a 2½ volt bulb. The bulb will be marked 2.5 V. just above the screw.

To make the *electric circuit*, bare the ends of the wires with a pen-knife and fasten them to the screws of the bulb holder. Screw the bulb in firmly. Run the wires down inside the lighthouse—and under the crumpled paper or cloth which represents the sea. Scrape the other ends of the wires bare, and fasten one end tightly to one of the brass strips (called the *poles*) of the battery. When

you join the other wire to the other pole, the light will go on. You may have to clean the battery poles with sandpaper to make a really good connection.

The diagram at the side of this page shows the electric circuit.

Conducting Electricity

When you buy a bulb or battery, the man in the shop tests it. You can test bulbs and batteries yourself with a pair of scissors, as you see in the little picture.

In your lighthouse, the electricity went through the wires. When you test a bulb, current goes through the scissors. What else will a current go through? You can soon find out.

Make a simple electric circuit with a battery, a bulb in a bulb holder, and two lengths of thin wire. You can use the same bulb holder as with the lighthouse—or the one in the picture, which is described on the next page.

When the bulb is alight, cut one of the wires. The light will go out, because the circuit is now broken. Bare the ends of the wire where you have cut it.

Now put all sorts of things between the bared ends of the wire. With some things you will find that the bulb will light, and that with others it will not.

Make two lists; one of the things which *conduct electricity;* the other of the things which do not conduct electricity—and which are called *non-conductors* or *insulators.*

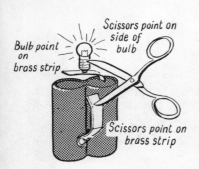

Scissors point on side of bulb

Bulb point on brass strip

Scissors point on brass strip

You will find that it is usually the metal articles which conduct electricity. But try the "lead" of a short piece of pencil in your circuit. You will probably get a faint glow in the bulb because although the "lead" of a pencil is not metal, it does conduct electricity.

Switch on and Switch off

You can fill the gap in the circuit in the last experiment with a switch. You need a piece of wood about the size of a match box, three drawing pins, a wire paper clip and two lengths of thin wire. First clean the tops of the drawing pins by rubbing them *hard* with a piece of sandpaper, so that they will make good connections.

The bared end of a wire is wound tightly round a drawing pin, the end of the paper clip is hooked round it, and the pin is pressed firmly into the wood. Another drawing pin, also with a wire wound round it, is pressed into the wood underneath, but not touching, the other end of the paper clip. A third drawing pin is put so that it will hold the clip down when you want to keep it switched on.

Another piece of wood, one drawing pin and a spring clothes-peg will make a bulb holder. The clothes-peg is nailed to the block, the bulb with a wire round it is clamped in the jaws, and under it is a drawing pin with the other wire under it. The bulb must be set so that it presses firmly on the head of the *cleaned* drawing pin.

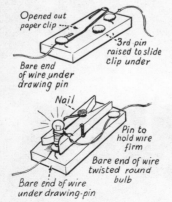

Opened out
paper clip ----

3rd pin
raised to slide
clip under

Bare end
of wire under
drawing pin

Nail

Pin to
hold wire
firm

Bare end of wire
twisted round
bulb

Bare end of wire
under drawing-pin

When the battery, switch and bulb are connected you can switch the bulb on and off by pressing the paper-clip.

You can signal to a friend by flashing your lights on and off. You can spell out words if you use the Morse code.

16

Electric Circuits

The children in the picture decided to fit electric lighting in their model theatre. They used three bulb holders for footlights, joining the wires from the bulb holders to the switch and battery.

When they pressed the switch, the bulbs only glowed very slightly. They checked the connections and tested the wire, the bulbs and the battery. Everything seemed to be right. Why did the bulbs only give a dim glow?

The reason was that the bulbs were connected one after the other—called *in series*. What they had to do was to connect the bulbs *in parallel*. You will understand "in series" and "in parallel" if you look carefully at the sketch at the bottom of this page.

When the bulbs were connected "in parallel" they all lit brightly—but this meant that the battery was being used up three times as fast. They fitted three more bulbs at the top of the stage, with wires to another switch and battery, and with all six bulbs switched on the stage was brilliantly lighted.

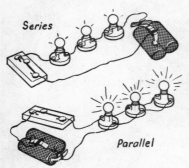

Series

Parallel

An Important Experiment

Early in the last century a Danish scientist named Oersted did a simple experiment which had far reaching results and made him famous among scientists. You can do the same experiment.

Magnetise a needle and place it on a piece of cork floating on water in a saucer. It will, of course, turn to a north-south direction. Hold a magnet near the needle and it will turn. Remove the magnet and it will return to the north-south direction.

Now connect a battery, a switch and about a foot of thin wire. Secure the wire across the top of the saucer with two dabs of plasticine, in the same direction as the needle. Make sure your connections are all good, and then switch on the current.

The needle will turn just as it did when the magnet was held near to it. What do you think this experiment shows?

When Oersted made the same experiment he realized it was an important discovery. It showed there was a

close connection between electricity and magnetism, because the electric current produced the same effect as the magnet. This was the beginning of the study of *electro-magnetism*, which led in time to the electric motor and the general use of electricity as a source of power.

An Electro Magnet

Magnets pick up certain things, and Oersted's experiment showed that a wire with an electric current passing through it had the same effect as a magnet. Will a wire with a current passing through it pick up things?

The answer is "Yes," but the magnetic effect is very weak. You can make a stronger magnet with a coil of wire and a nail.

Wind about fifty turns of thin wire round a three-inch nail, leaving the ends free. Connect them to a battery and a switch.

Without switching the current on, dip the end of the nail into some tin tacks. Now switch on. The nail will pick up a cluster of tacks. Switch off again, and the tacks will fall off. You have made an *electro-magnet*. A few tacks may stick to the nail when the current is switched off, because the nail itself has kept a little of its magnetism.

Now wind another fifty turns on to the nail, switch on and you will find that it has become an even stronger magnet.

If you wind the wire round a piece of steel, instead of iron, such as a steel screwdriver or a knitting needle,

and pass the current through the wire for a few seconds, the steel becomes permanently magnetised. This is how magnets are made. Do not keep your electro magnet switched on for more than a few seconds at a time, or your battery will quickly run down.

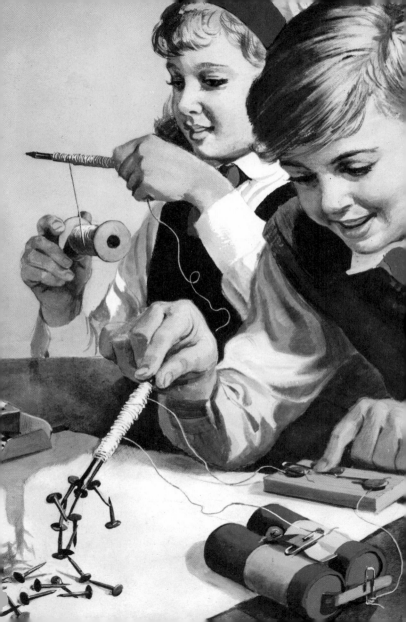

Magnetic Fields

Hold an ordinary magnet in each hand and bring them slowly together, and feel the push or pull. It seems that there is "something" round a magnet which we cannot see, but which affects another magnet, or a piece of iron or steel. That "something" is called a *magnetic field*.

You can do an interesting experiment if you get some iron filings, perhaps from an ironmonger, a garage, a workshop or your science teacher. Put them in a small tube with a screw cap. Make this into a sort of pepper-pot by punching small holes in the cap with a hammer and nail.

Lay a magnet on the table and cover it with a piece of white paper. Sprinkle some iron filings, from a good height so that they fall evenly round the covered magnet. Tap the paper *very gently* and watch how the iron filings arrange themselves. They will form lines and curves in an interesting pattern. Notice where these lines begin and end.

You can use two magnets, or three, changing their positions and seeing the different patterns they make.

Do the same experiment with your electro-magnet. Do not switch on until the filings are sprinkled and you are ready to tap the paper. Tap and switch off quickly.

The patterns formed by the filings give you an idea of the shape of the *magnetic fields* around the magnets.

Making a Signal—1

You can use an electro-magnet to work a toy signal. The signal is a piece of wood about seven inches long, half-an-inch wide and about a quarter-inch thick. The base-board is about four inches by two. The post is fixed into the base-board, either by making a hole and glueing, or by sticking it into a piece of plasticine. The signal arm is cut from stiff card or balsa wood, and painted in the usual way. Make two pin-holes at the points marked A and B in the diagram.

Now for the electrical part. Make a tube from a piece of sticky-paper two inches wide and about eight inches long, by rolling it on a pencil. Do not damp the sticky side for the first turn, or the pencil won't come out. Once you have made a complete turn lick the sticky paper.

You need about three-and-a-half yards of thin insulated wire to put about a hundred turns round the tube. Leave the pencil through the tube, and slip an elastic band over the end of the tube to keep the wire in place while you are winding it. Before you start winding the wire, leave about nine inches free to make the connection. When you finish winding smoothly and evenly, leave another length of nine inches and slip it under the elastic band with the other loose end. Bare both free ends of wire, draw out the pencil and there you have the coil for your electric signal.

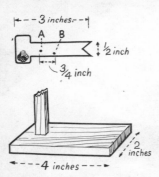

26

Making a Signal—2

Fix the signal arm to the post with a drawing pin through the hole at A (page 26), so that the arm moves freely. It will drop down. Now you need a nail which will go easily inside the paper tube. Fasten a length of cotton to the head of the nail with a dab of plasticine, as shown in the diagram. The other end of the cotton is tied to the signal arm through the hole at B (page 26). Balance the signal arm in the level position by putting plasticine at the back of the arm as in the diagram.

When the signal arm is balanced it will only require a small pull on the nail to bring it down, and this is done by the electro-magnet.

Mount the coil on the base-board so that the tip of the nail hangs freely just inside the coil. Move the coil to the right position and fix it on the base-board with plasticine.

You now make an electric circuit with a battery, a switch and your coil, connecting it as shown in the

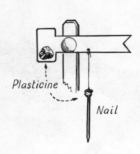

Plasticine

Nail

picture. When you switch on, the nail should be pulled down into the coil, bringing the signal arm down with it. When you switch off it should return to the level position. You may have to adjust the position of the coil slightly to make the signal work really well.

Detecting Electric Current

How can you detect an electric current in a wire? The answer is found in Oersted's experiment on page 20. The wire was fixed across a saucer of water, and when the current flowed the needle turned. Now wind the wire *right round* the saucer once only, and join it to a battery, bulb and switch. When you press the switch the bulb will light and the needle will turn. Notice how far it turns.

You made an electro-magnet by winding wire round an iron nail; the more turns of wire, the stronger it was. Wind about ten turns of wire round the saucer instead of one. Again connect the wire to the battery, bulb and switch. Switch on; the bulb will light, but notice the change in the movement of the needle. The more turns you put round the saucer the stronger the magnetic field and therefore the more the needle turns.

You have made an instrument for detecting electricity. Another way is to use a pocket compass. This time it is the compass needle which moves.

This kind of instrument is called a *galvanometer*, an electric current measurer. *Galvani* was an Italian scientist of 200 years ago who made some early discoveries in electricity. *Meter* means measure, and so—*galvanometer*.

Batteries

What are batteries made of? You can find out by taking an old one to pieces. First take off the cardboard wrappings, and you will find two metal containers joined by a short wire. These are called *cells*, and the two cells make a *battery*.

Tear off some of the zinc-casing of one of the cells with a pair of pliers. Inside you will see a jelly-like substance round a soft black sticky powder. Now grip the brass cap at the top tightly with the pliers. A firm twisting pull will draw out a black rod made of carbon.

The carbon rod and the zinc case are the *poles* of the cell. The white jelly and the black powder are chemicals which cause electricity to flow when the poles are joined. Do not get this on your hands or clothes, and if you *do* touch it, wash your hands.

Wash the strip of zinc you tore from the cell casing and clean it with sandpaper. Twist one end over and fix a wire to it. If you can borrow a juicy lemon, cut a slit in it and push the zinc well in. Cut another slit close by and push in the carbon rod.

Test a small, cycle lamp battery, never a large one,

with the tip of your tongue, as in the diagram; you will feel a slight tickling because your tongue is conducting electricity. Now try the same experiment with the zinc and brass cap of the carbon rod stuck into a lemon. If you feel a faint tickling on your tongue it is because an electric current has been produced by the action of the acid in the lemon.

Joining Batteries

The battery you have been using is a 3 volt torch battery. A battery "pushes" electric current round a circuit, and the number of *volts* marked on the battery tells you how much "push" a battery can give. If you join two batteries together you double the "push", which makes a bulb burn brighter.

Try this experiment with three 1½ volt batteries and a 3½ volt bulb (it may be marked 3.5 V). There are no brass strips on these batteries, so you wind the bared end of one wire tightly round the brass cap, and push the bared end of the other wire up between the cardboard and the zinc case, at the bottom of the battery. Connect *one* battery to a switch and the bulb. There will only be a dim glow.

Now put another battery in the circuit, joining the two batteries as in the picture. Try the light again. Then put in a third battery, connecting it again in series, and the bulb will light brightly.

The three batteries give you three times 1½ volts, which is 4½ volts. This "push" lights the bulb properly and is quite safe to handle. But the "push" from the electricity in your home is about 240 volts. This can be *very dangerous* and you must never interfere with mains electricity. The wires on pylons carry electricity at very high voltages indeed, up to 132,000 volts.

DANGER
132 000
VOLTS

An Electric Motor—I

The powerful electric motors which drive trains, trolley-buses and machinery in workshops and factories are very complicated. But you can make a simple electric motor yourself, which works the same way.

You will need a horseshoe magnet with a gap of about an inch between the poles. If you have not got one, try asking an ironmonger, a garage or a scrap-iron merchant. You will also need a cork about three-quarters of an inch long, some pins, a long darning needle, some thin wire and a few drawing pins.

There are two main parts to an electric motor; the part that spins round, called the *armature*, and the mounting. Begin with the armature.

Put the darning needle right through the middle of the cork from end to end. Take care not to prick yourself, and be sure that it goes *exactly* through the middle. Spin it between your fingers to make sure.

Now wind the wire on the cork. Put in the two pins as in the diagram, the same distance on each side of the needle, leaving about half-an-inch sticking out. You will use about four feet of thin insulated wire. Bare one end and wrap it firmly round one of the pins to make a good connection. Then wind the rest of the wire firmly round and round the cork as in the diagram.

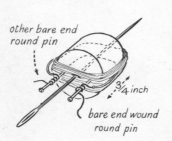

other bare end round pin

¾ inch

bare end wound round pin

When you come to the end of the wire, bare it and finish by twisting it round the other pin. You have now made the armature for your electric motor.

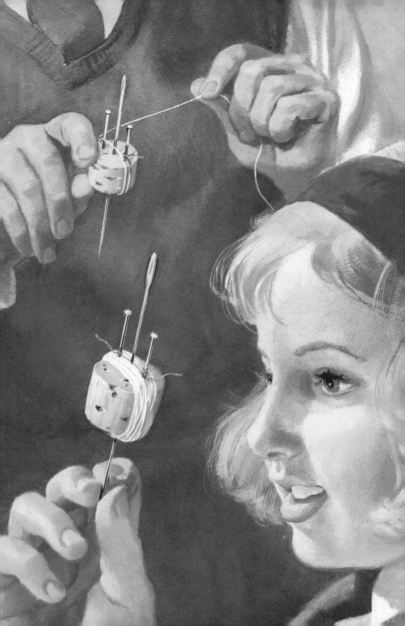

An Electric Motor—2

To make the mounting for your electric motor use a piece of wood about six inches long and three inches wide, and soft enough to push pins into it. The armature runs on two pairs of crossed pins set up along the middle of the block, far enough apart for the armature to spin freely. Two small strips of card in blobs of plasticine will stop the needle sliding backwards and forwards.

Next fix the two wires which take the current to the armature. These are called *brushes*, because they *brush* against the two pins as the armature spins round. The brushes are the bared ends of wires which stick up and are held in place by two drawing pins in your board. The other ends of these wires are connected to the poles of your torch battery.

To complete the motor put a magnet over the armature as shown in the diagram, and give it a spin to start it off. It should continue to spin as long as the wires are connected to the battery.

This motor will work, but it may not go first time. It needs a fairly strong magnet, and a second battery will help. You may have to spend a little time experimenting with the brushes, bending them to find the best position, so that they touch both pins firmly at the same time. It may be a good thing, when you have made the motor, to ask Father to try it.

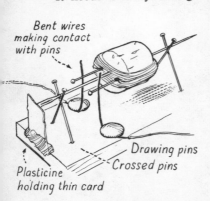

Bent wires making contact with pins

Drawing pins
Crossed pins

Plasticine holding thin card

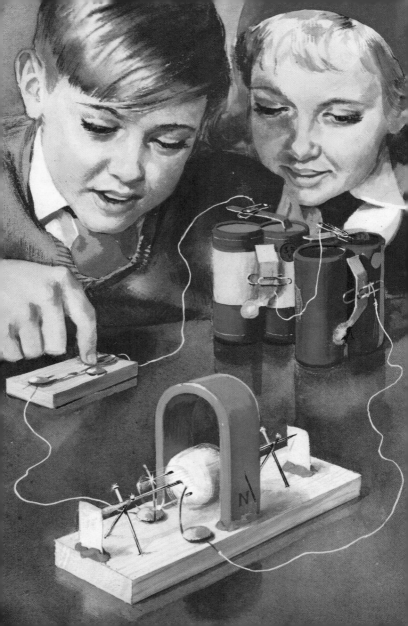

Electro-Plating

For this experiment you need some *copper sulphate* crystals. Half an ounce will only cost a few pence at the chemist or ironmonger. If you should get any on your fingers, wash your hands at once.

Dissolve some of the crystals in water in a small jar. This will produce a deep blue liquid.

Clean an iron nail carefully with emery paper, join a wire to it, and connect the other end of the wire to a battery. It is important, however, to connect the wire to the correct pole of the battery.

There is a difference between the two poles. The one at the top is called the *positive pole*, and is sometimes marked $+$. The pole at the side is the *negative pole*, and is sometimes marked $-$. The wire from your nail must be joined to the *negative pole*.

Connect another wire to the *positive pole* of the battery, and put the other end—carefully bared—into the liquid. Hang the nail in the liquid by bending the wire over the edge of the jar. Watch carefully to see what happens to the nail.

After a short while the part of your nail which is in the liquid will be coated with a thin layer of copper. It has been *copper-plated* by electricity; this is called *electro-plating*. The same method, using different liquids, is used for chromium plating, silver plating, gold-plating and so on.

Fuses and Short Circuits

Wherever electricity is used there are *fuses*. These are short pieces of special wire put into electrical circuits, so if anything goes wrong the wire gets hot, melts and breaks the circuit, so switching off the current.

You can find out how a fuse works by a simple experiment. Join three $1\frac{1}{2}$ volt batteries in series and connect them to a switch. Put the free ends under two drawing pins on a board about an inch apart, with the bared ends sticking up about an inch.

Your fuse is made from a very narrow strip of thin silver paper just over an inch long. With the switch off wind the ends of your fuse round the bared wires. Switch on and the fuse should get red hot and melt. If the fuse does not "blow", make it shorter.

Fuses usually blow because there is a *short circuit*, which means that the current is taking a "short cut" and not going the way it should.

Put a bulb and bulb-holder in your circuit, and join the ends of the wire with a silver paper fuse as before. Switch on and the bulb will light and the fuse will not blow. Now switch off and bare a short length of the wire on each side of the bulb holder. Switch on and make a *short circuit* by joining the bare patches with a piece of wire or a nail. The bulb will go out, and because you have made a short circuit the fuse will blow and the current will stop flowing.

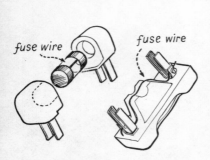

fuse wire

fuse wire

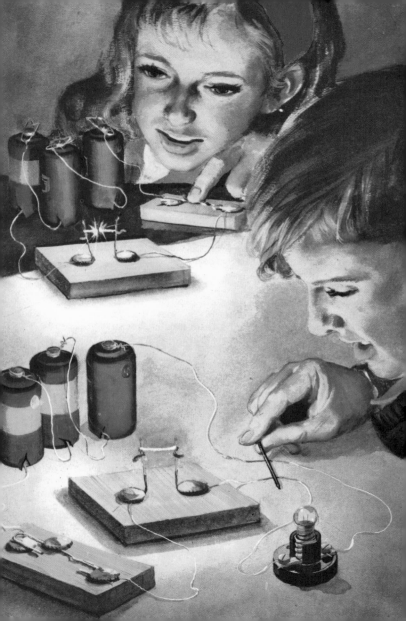

Electricity from Magnetism

When you passed an electric current through a wire, in Oersted's experiment on page 20, you made a floating magnet move. Can you imagine the *opposite*? If you move a magnet near a wire, do you get an electric current in the wire?

The answer is "Yes", but the current would be so very small that it could only be measured by a special instrument. The first man to ask himself this question, and to find the answer, was the great English scientist Michael Faraday, who lived a hundred years ago. Faraday experimented and found that when he moved a magnet near a wire a current was produced. From this discovery he continued experimenting, and his work led to the invention of the *dynamo*.

You cannot make a dynamo, but you may have one on your bicycle to provide electric current to light the lamps. When the dynamo is working you will notice that you have to pedal a little harder, because you cannot get electricity for nothing. You have to "pay" in one way or another.

If you can get an old cycle dynamo which is no longer any use, take it to pieces. You may need some help to start you off. Inside the dynamo you will find a

strange shaped, but very strong magnet which spins round close to the ends of several coils of wire. It is made to spin by a small wheel which presses against the cycle tyre. The spinning magnet close to the coils produces electricity in the coils, which lights the lamps.

44

Electric Light

You click down a switch, and the light comes on! It is so simple that we take it for granted. But what does happen when you switch on the electric light?

Ask someone to show you an electric light bulb with clear glass. At the bottom you will see two blobs of solder. These are the contacts with the bulb-holder. You will also see two wires which go up into the bulb, joined at the top to a ring of very thin wire. That is the *filament* and it is made of a special metal called *tungsten*. When this is heated by the electric current it becomes white hot and gives off a bright light.

You can make a simple electric light bulb. You need very thin iron wire, so look round for some picture wire, which is made of a number of strands. Use about two inches of a single strand.

Cut a piece of thick cardboard to make a cap for a small bottle. Press two nails through and fix your filament to the points. Fix the cardboard on the bottle. Join the wires to the heads of the nails, and to a switch and two batteries connected in series.

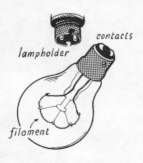

contacts

lampholder

filament

When you switch on the filament should glow red hot. You may have to experiment to find the right length of wire for the filament, but let it cool before you touch it. It will burn away quickly, but a real bulb contains a special gas, to stop the filament burning away.

Static Electricity

Tear up some thin tissue paper and drop the pieces on the table. Rub a plastic pen briskly against the sleeve of your coat or jersey, and bring it near the pieces of paper. They will jump up and stick to the pen. It seems rather like the tin tacks and magnet, but you know that plastic and paper are not magnetic. What is the cause?

This is *Static Electricity*, or electricity at rest. Your other experiments have been made with electricity flowing round a circuit; that is called *current electricity*.

When you rub the pen on your sleeve—or you could use a comb instead—the pen and sleeve become *charged* with static electricity. When you brush your hair hard with a plastic brush in dry weather, the brush and your hair become charged; sometimes you hear it crackle, and in the dark you might see sparks. When you stroke a cat's back in dry weather you sometimes get sparks.

You can "charge" balloons with static electricity. Blow them up, rub them on your sleeve, and they will stick to the wall or ceiling until they have lost their charge.

Rub the body of a ball point pen against your sleeve, and put it close to a very fine stream of water from the tap. The water will bend away from the pen because the pen is charged with static electricity.

Moving air can charge clouds to several *million* volts, and the spark produced when a cloud loses its charge to another cloud, or to earth, is lightning. The "crackle" made by this tremendous spark is thunder.

Electricity—Man's Servant

Think for a moment how different your life would be without electricity. Imagine what it would be like with no electric light in your home or school, or in the streets; no electric traffic lights, or electric trains. Your mother would not be able to have an electric cooker, electric fire, refrigerator, or any other modern help.

The wonderful work of the hospitals would be much more difficult without X-rays and other electrical instruments. Without electricity you would have no telephone, cinema, radio or television. Look carefully at the picture and see how many ways electricity is used there.

None of these things existed a hundred years ago. It was in 1860 that Sir Joseph Swan invented the electric lamp. Although the electric motor and electro-magnet had been invented about thirty years before that, they were not in everyday use until very much later. It was

just over a hundred years ago that the great Michael Faraday made his discoveries, for which we call him "the Father of Electricity."

When you think of the many ways electricity helps us in our daily life you will see why we must understand it. But remember, *never touch* mains electricity.

50

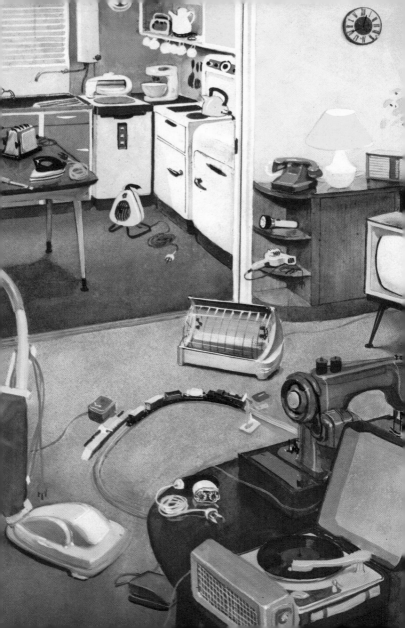

Here is a list of the few article
you will need for the experiment
in this book. You will probabl_
have most of them.

Batteries—1½ and 3 volt.

Torch bulbs—2½ and 3½ volt.

A bulb holder.

Connecting wire. Thin wir
covered with cotton, silk o
enamelled. Size "28 standar_
wire gauge" or nearest. An ol_
transformer from a radio sho_
will provide all the wire yo_
need—and more.

A bar magnet. A horse-sho
magnet.